Cold Cold Heart

Mike Gould

Folens

United Kingdom: Folens Publishers, Apex Business Centre, Boscombe Road, Dunstable, LU5 4RL.
Email: folens@folens.com

Ireland: Folens Publishers, Greenhills Road, Tallaght, Dublin 24.
Email: info@folens.ie

Poland: JUKA, ul. Renesansowa 38, Warsaw 01-905.

Editor: Joanne Mitchell

Layout artist: Suzanne Ward

Cover design: John Hawkins

First published 2005 by Folens Limited.

British Library Cataloguing in Publication Data. A catalogue record for this publication is available from the British Library.

ISBN 1 84303 734 3

Contents

The story so far

If you haven't read an *On the edge* book before:
The stories take place in and around a row of shops and buildings called Pier Parade in Brightsea, right next to the sea. There's Big Fry, the fish and chip shop; Drop Zone, the drop-in centre for local teenagers; Macmillan's, the sweet and souvenir shop; Anglers' Haven, the fishing tackle shop; the Surf 'n' Skate shop and, of course, the Brightsea Beach Bar.

If you have read an *On the edge* book you may have met some of these people before.

Miss Dedlock: *owner of Dedlock's Loan Agency.*

Jason Hillman: *a young 'gangster'.*

Greg Davy: *grandson of Charlie Davy, owner of the fishing shop.*

Sam Roberts: *his best friend.*

So, what's been going on?
Jason led Sam into all sorts of mischief, along with London gangster, Ray, but that's all in the past. Jason has been excluded from school and Sam doesn't see him anymore. Meanwhile, Mel almost lost his bar to the Dedlocks to whom he owed money, until he paid them off at the last minute.

What happens in this story?
Jason has been excluded from school and feels isolated. His dad doesn't want to know him and his mum is a prisoner in her own home, with no sense of purpose. Jason wants to do something, anything – legal or illegal – and along comes Miss Dedlock, owner of a loan agency, with some dodgy business she needs doing. But Jason has to face much worse than her, when he confronts his own father …

Characters

JASON HILLMAN: aged 15

MRS HILLMAN: Jason's mother

JEFF HILLMAN: Jason's father

MISS DEDLOCK: owner of a loan agency

MEL SLATER: owner of the 3 Bs

MAN: the 'rat-catcher'

GREG DAVY: a schoolboy

SAM ROBERTS: Greg's friend

POLICE OFFICER

Scene 1

Dedlock's office.

Late afternoon.

A pale, thin, hard-looking woman behind a desk. It is Miss DEDLOCK, owner of Dedlock's Loan Agency. In front of her stands JASON, a young man.

DEDLOCK: What do you want?

JASON: You sent for me.

DEDLOCK: I never send for people.

JASON: I'll go then …

DEDLOCK: Wait. Who told you to come here?

JASON: One of your brothers …

DEDLOCK: What my brothers do is no concern of mine.

JASON: But they said …

DEDLOCK (*interrupting*):
Never mind what they said. They say lots of things – most of them not worth listening to.

JASON: They seemed alright to me.

DEDLOCK: Yes – they can appear quite normal sometimes. Funny, how appearances can deceive.

JASON: They bought me drinks. Gave me some cigarettes.

DEDLOCK: Very generous of them. Hope it wasn't my money.

JASON: I can give the cigarettes back …

DEDLOCK waves the offer away, then stands up and moves to the window.

DEDLOCK: Why are you here?

JASON (*uncertainly*):
   I thought you might …

DEDLOCK (*turning round*):
   Spit it out!

JASON: Need someone.

DEDLOCK: For what?

JASON: I dunno. Thought you could tell me that.

DEDLOCK: How helpful. You come here, offering to help, but you don't know what you can do.

JASON: Look, someone …

DEDLOCK: Someone?

JASON: I have ears too.

DEDLOCK: Very observant. Continue.

JASON: What I mean is, I was told the cops were on your back. Making it difficult to do business … (*pauses*)

DEDLOCK: Go on. I'm listening.

JASON: I thought you might need someone to help you.

DEDLOCK: Help me?

JASON: You know – get your money back. I mean, that's what you do, isn't it? Lend money to people, then get it back.

DEDLOCK: Problem is, they don't pay on time. People are greedy.

JASON: That's where I come in. I could force them to pay. You know … go round there … smash a few things …

DEDLOCK (*interrupts*):

Enough! Do you think we're animals? No – I run a legitimate business. What we do is *encourage* them to pay. They might need a little reminder, certainly. They might have to give us something – a television, some jewellery … until they can pay. But let's have no more talk of smashing, or breaking …

JASON: But your brothers said …

DEDLOCK: They're idiots. If it wasn't for me, this business would have fallen apart years ago. No, we need a new approach now. You don't stand out – not like those big, ugly brothers of mine.

JASON: What's in it for me?

DEDLOCK: For you? Well, you've been kicked out of school …

JASON: How did you know that?

DEDLOCK: What was it? Drugs?

JASON: No way. They're for losers.

DEDLOCK: Violent behaviour, then …

JASON: I never hurt anyone …

DEDLOCK: Carrying an offensive weapon, perhaps …

JASON: Yeah. That was it – a knife. So what? Everyone has one nowadays. Anyway, how did you know?

DEDLOCK: Never you mind. Kicked out of school … you're without a job. And I hear things aren't so great at home.

JASON: Home? What do you know about that?

DEDLOCK (*mimics JASON*):
'I have ears'. Yes, home life isn't too good, is it?

JASON: I don't want to have anything to do with that dump.

DEDLOCK: Exactly. I might be able to find you a room somewhere – throw in some money – when you prove yourself.

JASON: Prove myself?

DEDLOCK: Yes – you know, see if you're up to the job.

JASON: I've done stuff. Stuff I could tell you about.

DEDLOCK: Don't worry, I already know. And you weren't terribly good at it, were you?

JASON: It weren't my fault that gang from London came after me and Ray.

DEDLOCK: Oh yes, Ray the big gangster. What happened to him?

JASON: Dunno – he just sort of disappeared.

DEDLOCK: Let's hope it's permanent. The point is, your track record isn't covered with glory. You need to be a bit more classy. Move upmarket. Keep away from nasty people like Ray and that London gang.

JASON: That's what I want. Just give me a chance.

DEDLOCK: Not so eager. There's no rush. There'll be plenty of time for you to make your mark.

JASON: So, you'll use me?

DEDLOCK: We'll see. Let's just discuss terms and conditions first.

Scene 2

Jason's parents' flat.

Early evening.

The lounge. There's a coffee table with a full ashtray on it. The TV flickers in the corner. A cat is spread out on the rug. The place is generally untidy. On the mantelpiece are several dusty framed photos of happier times. The curtains are drawn. Enter JASON. His MUM follows. She is wearing slippers and a dressing gown, even though it is late afternoon.

JASON: Is he here?

MUM: No, love. Don't worry. You and I can have a nice little chat. Watch the telly. *Millionaire* is on later.

JASON: I'm not staying.

MUM: What d'you mean?

JASON: I'm moving out.

MUM (*sinks onto sofa*):
         Is it him?

JASON: What do you think?

MUM: But why? You used to get on
         just great.

JASON: Funny enough, I think him
         battering me every time I
         said anything out of line had
         something to do with it.

MUM: He didn't mean it.

JASON: Still hurts the same whether
         someone means it or not.

MUM: But you stand up to him now.
         You don't let him do that
         anymore.

JASON: Just 'cos it don't happen now,
         doesn't mean I don't remember
         it. You don't see it, do you?
         D'you think he whacked me
         'cos I was his fave little boy?
         Do you?

MUM: He's …

JASON: Proud of me? Is that what you
         were gonna say? 'Cos if you
         were, save it. It ain't true.

MUM: I was going to say he's
         depressed.

JASON: My heart bleeds.

MUM: Don't be like that.

*JASON goes over to the curtains and pulls
them open.*

JASON: Can't see a thing in this place. Here. (*flings two packets of cigarettes onto the table*) Your type, aren't they?

MUM: Ta, love. Where d'you get them?

JASON: They were a gift.

MUM: Don't you want them?

JASON: They make my clothes stink. I have to look smart and sharp. It don't do to look out of place in my line of work.

MUM (*excited*):
          You got a job?

JASON: Well, I'm not going back to school, am I?

MUM: You can help me out now then. With the rent and all that. 'Cos I need a bit of help. Things have been hard now your dad's out of work.

JASON: He was always out of work.

MUM: He's out looking for a job now.

JASON: Yeah. I bet he's asked in every pub in town.

MUM reaches out her hand and touches JASON's arm.

MUM: Don't leave your mum alone.

JASON: You've got him.

MUM: I did have.

JASON: What d'you mean?

MUM: He's moving out.

JASON: He'll be back.

MUM: This time I think he means it.
He's taken the money from the
tin.

JASON: I gave you that! From that job I
did in the summer.

MUM: Don't be angry. He needs it
more than me.

JASON sits on the table opposite her.

JASON: Why d'you stand up for him?
What's he ever done for us?

MUM: He loves you …

JASON: Maybe once. Not after …

MUM: I don't want to talk about it.

JASON (*hard*):

> No – that's right. Don't talk about it. The awful truth. Well, don't worry. You won't have to think about it. 'Cos I won't be here to remind you. (*gets up*)

MUM: Where you going?

JASON: Get my stuff. What's left of it.

MUM: Don't leave!

JASON (*more gentle*):

> I have to, mum. You see – I've got nothing.

MUM: You have me, son.

JASON: How can I stay here? Is this all there is? Stuck here watching you smoke yourself to death?

MUM: I'll give up.

JASON: It's not the smoking. That's just an example.

MUM: I don't understand.

JASON: Look, mum – I've always been a loser. But now I've got this chance. I promise I'll come and see you.

MUM: I don't wanna be left with him.

JASON (*changes tone*):
          I thought you said he was gone?

MUM: I said that 'cos I thought you might stay.

JASON: You mean he's coming back? When?

MUM doesn't answer.

JASON (*angry*):
> Tell me!

MUM: Any minute.

JASON: You stupid … (*breaks off*) I'm going. If I stay here I'll do something to him. Something I'll regret.

MUM: You wouldn't hurt your own father, would you?

JASON: Wouldn't I? Look, I'll pop back for my things another time.

MUM: You don't want to see him?

JASON (*turns as he reaches the door*):
> I don't ever want to see him again.

Scene 3

The seafront.

The next day.

SAM is on his skateboard. GREG is on a bike.

GREG: Oi, slow down. I'm not as quick as you.

SAM: You've got your bike.

GREG: It's got a slow puncture.

SAM: So? You should have brought your board.

GREG: I'm not good enough yet.

SAM: You need to practise then.

GREG: OK. You've made your point. Anyway, the reason I was left behind was *not* because of the puncture.

SAM: What was it then?

GREG: It's 'cos I saw an old friend of yours.

SAM: Who?

GREG: That Jason.

SAM: Jason? He was kicked out of school months ago. I thought he'd moved away or something.

GREG: Don't think so. His mum and dad still live up on Aldmoor Estate.

SAM: So, what's he up to? I need to keep clear of him – he was trouble.

GREG: Actually, he looked kind of smart. He had a leather jacket on and I think he had some sort of briefcase.

SAM: You're kidding? Jason becomes respectable. Don't think so. Where d'you see him?

GREG: Outside the 3 Bs. He didn't go
          in – he was just looking at it.

SAM: So that means he's coming our
          way?

GREG: Yeah. You wanna turn round?

SAM: No – I got to face him
          sometime. Might as well be
          now.

*At that moment JASON appears round the
corner. He sees them and stops.*

SAM: Jason.

JASON: What you up to, Sam? What
          you doing with lover-boy here?

SAM: Lover-boy?

JASON: You're like husband and wife.
          You should get married.

SAM: Greg's a mate.

JASON: Like we were mates.

SAM: That's all over. Last summer.

JASON: Yeah – you let me down bad.

SAM: I never let you down. I should never have got involved with you.

JASON: Still – as you say. It's all over now. Water under the bridge. But we could have been good together, me and you.

SAM: I don't think so.

JASON: Don't matter now. I don't need you. I'm well set.

SAM: Doing alright then?

JASON: Could say that. Anyway, got things to do, people to see. You know something? You wanna ditch that loser. You ever decide you need something, give me a call. Here's my mobile number.

JASON reaches out, grabs SAM's hand and turns it over. Then he scribbles on it with a pen he's pulled from his leather jacket.

JASON:　See you around, Sam. Stay smart – stay pretty.

JASON strolls off.

GREG:　Nasty piece of work. Why was he kicked out of school?

SAM:　Had a knife, or something. Funny thing is, I used to be frightened of him. Now … I don't know.

GREG:　Don't tell me you feel sorry for him!

SAM:　I dunno. Can't put it into words.

GREG:　It was dead weird how he spoke, wasn't it?

SAM: Yeah. Like he was kind of jealous or something.

GREG: Probably 'cos of last summer and that stuff with you, him and Ray.

SAM: Maybe. Anyway, long as he keeps out of my way, I'll keep out of his.

GREG: Yeah. Good thinking.

SAM: OK – come on. I'll race you.

GREG: Race me? I've got a flat tyre.

SAM: Well, that should even things up. Me on a board, you on half a bike.

SAM sets off.

GREG: Hey. Wait up! That's not fair …

Scene 4

The seafront.

Late at night.

JASON on the phone. He has a large canvas bag with him.

JASON: Yeah. I know what to do.

JASON ends the call and slips the mobile into his pocket. He goes up to the front of the 3 Bs, then glances over his shoulder. By the side of the bar are some bins. JASON opens the bag.

JASON: Go on then.

Nothing much happens.

JASON: Don't you get it? You're free …

JASON shakes the bag again. This time there's some movement.

JASON: Yeah – that's it! Lovely grub
          – go on …

JASON closes the bag, looks around and then starts jogging off.

Scene 5

Outside the 3 Bs.

Early next day.

MEL and a MAN in a boiler suit are standing outside the bar. There is a large box on one of the tables.

MAN: Well – we got 'em.

MEL: Thank God for that. Would have been terrible for business.

MAN: Not really.

MEL: What do you mean 'not really'?! Two rats are found near my premises? I run a bar. I have food here. Who's going to want to eat and drink in a place with rats?

MAN: I would.

MEL: Yes – but you're a rat-catcher. You *like* rats.

MAN: I wouldn't go that far. I'd say I *understand* rats. We speak the same language.

MEL: Maybe. But the truth is, most people can't stand them. And certainly not in a bar.

MAN: As I said, it's not really a problem.

MEL: What do you mean?

MAN: Didn't anything strike you as strange about those two rats?

MEL: Well, they weren't much good at hiding. I saw them straight away.

MAN: Exactly. They're not your average wild, common rats. Oh no. These two came from some pet shop. They're exotic.

MEL: 'Exotic'?

MAN: From some other country. Syria,
         Russia, South America … poor
         things looked pleased when I
         caught them. They're used to
         regular feeding and a warm
         cage.

MEL: So, they escaped from someone's
         house?

MAN: I doubt it. Two of them? Seems a
         bit unlikely. No – I'd look closer
         to home. Is there anyone you've
         upset who wanted to get back at
         you?

MEL: No – course not. Nobody …
         (*breaks off*) actually, now you
         mention it.

MAN: There you are, then. Right, I'll be
         off.

He holds up the box/container.

MAN: Say 'Goodbye' to the nice man!

He walks off and goes up the steps towards the road.

Scene 6

Dedlock's office.

Later that day.

MEL is in front of Miss DEDLOCK's desk.

MEL: It was you, wasn't it?

DEDLOCK: I have no idea what …

MEL: Don't give me that! Ever
            since you tried – and failed
            – to get the bar from me
            you've been looking for a
            way to get back at me.

DEDLOCK: What exactly are you
            accusing me of?

MEL: In a word, 'rats'.

DEDLOCK: Rats? Cuddly, brown things
            with sharp teeth?

MEL: You know exactly what I
            mean! You sent one of your
            cronies out at night, probably
            one of your brothers, and
            they set them free. It was
            lucky for me that you or they
            chose the most gentle rats on
            earth. We found them before
            they burrowed their way
            into the bar.

DEDLOCK: That must have been a relief,
            Mr Slater. Now, if you'll
            excuse me, I have to get on.
            Still, if you do decide the bar
            is getting too much for you, I
            could offer you a very decent
            price.

MEL: I'll never sell to you.

DEDLOCK: We'll see. Perhaps it won't be
            rats next time.

MEL: Are you threatening me?

DEDLOCK: Of course not. I'm much
            too clever to do anything
            obvious like that. Goodbye.

*She gets up and opens the door. MEL storms
out. She goes to another door and opens it.*

DEDLOCK: You can come in. He's gone.

JASON emerges.

JASON: He was pretty mad.

DEDLOCK: And so am I.

JASON: What – with him?

DEDLOCK: Not with him. You!

JASON: Me?

DEDLOCK: I didn't expect you to plant
            cuddly, little pet rats at the
            bar. I expected great, big,
            nasty ones bringing disease
            and death.

JASON: Death?

DEDLOCK: You know what I mean.

JASON: I couldn't get any of them.
            They only had the little
            ones. I didn't want to let you
            down.

DEDLOCK: Well, you did. If you want to
            get paid – and keep that little
            room I'm paying for – you're
            going to have to do better
            than that.

JASON: I will. Just tell me what to
            do.

DEDLOCK: This one's a real test. If you
            can do this, then you can do
            anything.

JASON: Whatever. I'll do it.

DEDLOCK: Alright. Here's the deal.

She passes an envelope across the desk.

DEDLOCK: Take it with you. In it is the address of someone who owes me some money. They haven't paid for months. I want you to go round there and get my money. If you don't get it, you're finished here. No job, no room, no future. I don't care how you make them pay, just don't get caught. And if you can't sort them out – we'll do it and it won't be pretty. Once you've opened the note and read the address – and how much is owed, I want you to destroy it. OK?

JASON: OK. I can do that.

DEDLOCK: Good. And remember you need to have a cold heart for this business. These people who owe money are spongers. They're weak. They'll do anything to get out of paying. Don't let them get to you. Remember what I said. A cold heart. You can't go wrong.

Scene 7

The street outside Dedlock's office.

A few moments later.

JASON tears open the envelope. He reads it. As he does so, a look of horror comes over his face.

JASON: I don't believe it! First, rats.
Now this.

He reads it again and tears it in half, then throws the two pieces on the ground. Then he strides off. He doesn't see MEL come out of the shadows. He goes over to the first piece and picks it up. Then he finds the other one. He arranges them, then reads them to himself.

MEL: Your next victim, huh? We'll see about that.

Scene 8

Jason's parents' flat.

Early evening.

JASON enters.

JASON: Mum.

MUM gets up from the sofa.

MUM: Jason! You're back.

JASON: I'm not staying, so don't get any ideas.

MUM: Can I make you a drink, or some supper? Have you eaten?

JASON: I'm not hungry.

MUM: You must be hungry – look at the time. It's gone 7:00 pm.

JASON (*ignores her*):
He's not here is he?

MUM: No – he's gone out.

JASON: The pub.

MUM: Don't think so. Said he had a job interview.

JASON (*bitterly*):

Job interview! Mum – how come you don't see through him? He's been bleeding you dry – us dry – for years. That's why you owe so much money.

MUM: How d'you know how much we owe?

JASON: I just do.

MUM: Has that Paula next door been talking? She's a right nosy cow. Must have seen them take the TV away.

JASON: What?

MUM: Didn't you notice?

JASON looks for the first time at the space where the TV was.

MUM: It was a good one, too. Cost a packet.

JASON: Who took it?

MUM: Oh – no one you'd know. These two brothers.

JASON: I know them. Did they hurt you?

MUM: No. Your dad was here. They were laughing and joking together. He told them to take it. Said he didn't like TV anyway.

JASON: What about you? You like your programmes.

MUM: There's always the radio.

She moves towards the kitchen.

MUM: Now, how about that supper?

JASON: Mum!

She turns.

MUM: What is it, love? You seem
      awful jumpy.

JASON sits down.

JASON: You got to pay them back. Pay
        all the money you owe.

MUM: We'll find a way. I can borrow
      some more from someone else.
      I'll see someone next week.

JASON: No. That's too late.

MUM: What d'you mean?

JASON: You have to pay them now.

MUM: What d'you know about it?

JASON: I know the people who lent you
        the money. You can't mess with
        them. I need to take the money
        – pay them back for you.

MUM: Don't be daft. I haven't got it.

JASON turns and grasps his MUM's hands.

MUM: You're hurting!

JASON: I don't mean to. (*releases her*)
        There must be something. Some
        money. When gran died, didn't
        she leave you something?

MUM: It's all gone.

JASON gets up.

JASON (*desperate*):
        I have to get the money.
        Otherwise …

MUM: What?

JASON: I'll have nothing. I promised
        them. They're the ones who
        offered me a job.

MUM: A job? Scaring people into paying up. Call that a job?

JASON: It's something. At least I'm not useless, like him.

JASON points at the mantelpiece – at the photos. As he does so, a figure emerges from the hallway. It's JASON's DAD. He's slightly drunk.

DAD: Useless, eh? See what I got here?

JASON (*turning*):
         Dad!

DAD (*holds out his hand*):
         Look. Two hundred.

MUM: How d'you get that?

DAD: Never you mind. Let's just say your old mum's silver spoons came in handy.

MUM: Jeff! That was all she left me.

DAD: Us. She left it to us. What's
         mine is yours and all that. Like
         him. (*gestures at JASON*) He's
         mine.

JASON: You need to give me that
         money, dad.

DAD (*shouts*):
         What for? So you can spend it
         on that boyfriend of yours?

JASON: Boyfriend? What you on about?

DAD: Well – you're gay so you must
         have a boyfriend.

MUM: Jeff. Don't say such things!

JASON: It's true, mum. It's the only
         good thing in my life. But I
         haven't got a boyfriend.

DAD (*nasty*):

> Were you planning to bring him here for tea? Play happy families?

JASON: I wouldn't bring *anyone* here. Even if there was someone, which there isn't.

DAD: Well, that's just as well. 'Cos I don't even like talking to you, let alone any of your mates.

JASON: When I told you last year … I hoped you might at least understand. I mean, I like all the same things as you: football, silly comedies on telly … God, I even look like you. But, oh no … you thought you could beat it out of me. Like I'd chosen it.

DAD (*moves to the other side of the room. Picks up a photo of JASON from the mantelpiece*):

>You did choose it. To spite me.

JASON: You stupid fool. It chose me. Like I didn't choose to have your looks, I just got them. Anyway, forget me. But for mum's sake at least, you have to give me the money you owe.

DAD: For her sake?

JASON: You owe the money to the Dedlocks. And if you don't pay up, there's no future for you, mum or me. 'Cos they'll come calling – and it won't be the TV they want this time.

DAD: They're my mates. They won't make me pay up.

JASON: They will. And they won't be laughing and joking. Look, dad, just give me that money – and the rest.

DAD: The rest?

JASON: Those spoons were solid silver. Antiques.

DAD: And what …?

JASON: You'll never see me again. You won't have to put up with your gay son. I'll be out of your life. Forever.

DAD looks at the money. He slowly rolls off one note and lets it flutter to the ground.

DAD: There. That's all you're getting from me. Now, get out of my way. I'm going out again.

JASON: Give me the money!

DAD: What? So, you can spend it on girly clothes and perfume?

JASON: Is that what you think being gay is all about?

DAD: I don't care. Just get out of my way!

DAD starts moving towards JASON.

JASON: I'm warning you, dad!

DAD stops, looks up.

DAD: What?

JASON pulls a knife from his pocket and holds it in front of him. His hand is shaking. He is almost crying. At this point, unseen by them all, MEL has entered the room at the back, near the doorway. He watches the scene.

DAD: Don't you threaten me!

JASON: You're not going anywhere!

DAD makes a sudden rush to get past JASON. There's a scuffle and DAD falls to the ground. JASON looks down at the knife – it has blood on it.

MUM kneels on the floor.

MUM: You stabbed him. Your own
             father …

JASON (*looks from her to the figure on the
ground*):
             I had to …

MEL (*steps forward*):
             I'll call an ambulance.

MUM: Who are you?

MEL: Never mind that. Where's your
             phone?

MUM: Hall. Quick, please!

JASON turns and runs out of the flat.

Scene 9

The seafront.

Mid-evening.

SAM and GREG are walking. GREG is pushing his bike.

GREG: Not bad, those ramps.

SAM: It was alright. You should have brought your board.

GREG: I know.

Suddenly, JASON appears running. We hear the sound of sirens. He approaches them. Tears are running down his cheeks. There is blood on his shirt.

JASON (*desperate*):
　　　You have to help me!

SAM: What's going on? (*sees the blood*) You've got blood on you …

JASON looks down. He hasn't realised until now.

JASON: I didn't … I had to … the old fool wouldn't …

SAM: What have you done?

JASON: The police … they're after me. You got to help me!

SAM: What can we do?

JASON (*to GREG*):
Gimme your bike.

SAM: It's broken, man.

JASON: I got to get away. Please!

GREG: I can't …

SAM: Give him the bike, Greg.

GREG: What?

SAM: Give it to him!

GREG looks at both of them. Then passes the bike to JASON. The sirens get louder. JASON leaps onto the bike. He turns and faces them for a moment. Then he races off, skidding this way and that.

GREG: That was my bike.

SAM: It's only a bike.

GREG: What d'you think's going on?

SAM: Come on – let's go up to the road. That's where all the sirens are.

Scene 10

Road by the seafront.

Later.

A light flashes at the back of the stage, suggesting a police car. JASON is between two police officers. His hands are handcuffed in front of him. He looks at SAM and GREG, who have entered. JASON steps forward, away from the police officers.

JASON: They got your bike back there.

GREG walks off, past the police officers and off stage.

SAM: What happened?

JASON: My dad.

SAM: You hurt him?

JASON: They tell me he's alright. Just.

SAM: Thank God for that.

JASON: I wish I'd killed him … after
         what he said, what he did.

SAM: You don't mean that.

JASON: You know something, Sam?
         Stay cool, stay smart. You don't
         wanna end up like me.

SAM: I don't know you, Jason. You
         were just a kid at school I got
         mixed up with.

JASON: You're right. We weren't ever
         friends, were we?

SAM: I never thought about it till
         now.

POLICE OFFICER:
         Come on, son. We've got to go.

JASON remains facing SAM.

SAM: What's gonna happen now?

JASON: They're gonna lock me up.

SAM: They might not.

JASON: I would if I was them.

SAM: Not if it wasn't your fault.

JASON: Maybe.

SAM stays silent.

JASON: There's one thing I want you to do.

SAM: What's that?

JASON (*checks that the POLICE OFFICER isn't listening*):

Go down to the 3 Bs. I hid something by the door when I was being chased. It's money. Give it to that man, Mel. He'll know what it's for.

SAM: Right.

POLICE OFFICER comes forward.

JASON: I'll see you.

SAM: Yeah.

JASON: Remember what I said, pretty
          boy. Stay smart.

Glossary

(to) burrow	(to) dig with hands or paws into the ground or earth
(to) deceive	(to) trick into believing
(to) ditch someone	(to) stop seeing someone suddenly
(to) encourage	(to) offer praise and help
exotic	suggesting far-distant foreign lands
fave	favourite
grub	food (informal)
jumpy	nervous, anxious
legitimate	within the law
my heart bleeds	I have no sympathy (usually used to mean the opposite)
observant	having a good eye for something
offensive	liable to upset or cause harm
permanent	unchanging
puncture	hole in a tyre
quit	leave
respectable	well-regarded
sirens	sound device used by police and others
spit it out!	expression meaning 'Say what you want – don't hold back.'
spongers	people who unfairly rely on others' generosity
well set	in a good position